Thomas Edison

A Captivating Guide to the Life of a Genius Inventor

Contents

Free Bonus from Captivating History (Available for a Limited time)

Hi History Lover!

Now you have a chance to join our exclusive history list so you can get your first history ebook for free as well as discounts and a potential to get more history books for free! Simply visit the link below to join.

Captivatinghistory.com/ebook

Also, make sure to follow us on:

Twitter: @Captivhistory

Facebook: Captivating History:@captivatinghistory

Introduction

Thomas Edison was born into a hard-working but attentive family. He struggled in school and became deaf at an early age. Born on February 11, 1847, Edison would become, arguably, the best-known American inventor of all time. His invention of the light bulb was one of more than 1,000 patents he held during his lifetime. Others included the phonograph, the electrical grid, and motion pictures. His work changed the way we see and hear the world around us.

America Before Edison

The story of Thomas Edison begins in a spectacular social and political context. In the late 18th and early 19th century, North America was on the brink of the shift from upstart colonial outpost to full-fledged participant in world affairs. Truly the land of opportunity, at least for enterprising and well-connected European immigrants; the promise of freedom from political and religious oppression drew boatloads of hopeful settlers to points of entry including Pier 21 in Halifax, and Ellis Island in New York. Edison's great-grandparents arrived in America from Holland and Scotland, and would each have an impact on the development of the youngster who would come to possess one of the most famous names in the world. The place they made a home, smack in the center of the continent, provides a glimpse into some of the changes going on in the Americas and beyond.

Settled a handful of decades earlier by three pioneering families, Milan, Ohio hugs the Huron River near the merging of its eastern and western branches. It was an exciting place of rapid growth and one where a young, ambitious family could make a good start at success. One such family was the Edisons and among them, Thomas Alva, who would have a significant impact on the technological, innovation-driven revolution of the 20th century.

The earliest map of the Milan, Ohio region is from 1812 and shows

'Indian Trails' crisscrossing the area, a state road, and a dedicated military road to neighboring Medina County. Established in 1838, Erie County became associated with the Underground Railroad: ushering escaped slaves to freedom north of the border. By the middle of the 19th century, demand for slave labour had expanded westward from its beginnings on the eastern seaboard. Field hands were bringing close to $1,000, and slaveholders had no compunction about separating families for profit. Many slaves, not surprisingly, decided to take the chance at freedom presented by the friendly neighbor to the north, Canada. In 1833, Great Britain had outlawed slavery in Canada. Geography, among other factors, meant Ohio presented a key route for escape. Its southern river introduced a passable line between the free and slaveholding nations, depositing freedom-seekers only a few hundred miles from port cities like Cleveland. Ohio boasted naturally draining prime agricultural land and groves of ship-worthy timber that served the first settler families well. Even before settlers arrived on the scene, Moravian missionaries from Canada had set out to save souls in the area but decamped when settler roots started to take hold. Those first settlers, the Abbots, Wards, Walworths, and Parkers, began to farm and build, and although some of the original immigrants were displaced during the War of 1812, the town of Milan quickly became a community. Relations with the first inhabitants were sometimes cordial, and occasionally violent, but eventually developed into a grudging cooperation, much like relations between settlers and First Nations peoples in the rest of the young nation. The Eerie, Kickapoo, and Shawnee tribes were the original inhabitants of the area, but other tribes including Delaware, Miami, Wyandot, and the Ohio Seneca migrated to the area after the appearance of Europeans. Much of the animosity, on both sides, dissipated when Confederate soldiers stationed in the area left for their homes. Many aboriginal soldiers from the region participated in the conflict between Britain and France. During peacetime, single-room schoolhouses emerged, and various denominations of churches including; Presbyterian, Anglican, Episcopalian, and Lutheran, and as usually follows, a tavern, shoemaker, chemist and the rest of the necessities of settler life sprouted from the verdant land.

As in other pioneering towns with resources to spare, speculators soon arrived on the scene, and one of their chief interests was the construction of a canal to transport grains using barges to the Huron River and subsequently to schooners. Lake-going schooners were in regular use in other regions for delivering goods to major ports. Until the Milan Canal was constructed, Ohio farmers relied on rough and poorly placed roads, and as a result, made little headway in continental trade. Significant roads skirted the central part of the state to the north, south, and west, and left many Ohioan farmers virtually stranded.

One solution was to create a navigable waterway to ease transportation of people, livestock, and goods. The fledgling community supported the idea of a three-mile-long canal consisting of two locks, a dam, a tollhouse, and a mill. The original projected cost of $5,800 soon increased when the developers decided to make the canal deep enough to accommodate lake schooners, large vessels that had a presence on the Great Lakes since the 17th century. As one historian notes, "In the early 1860s, there were reportedly more than 750 canal schooners on the Lakes out of a total of nearly 1,300 sailing craft. The *canallers* were the backbone of the Great Lakes fleet." The final tally for the canal ($23,392) paid for itself in no time.

By 1840, and in large part due to its location near Lake Erie, Milan was becoming a critical grain shipping port. Shipbuilding was a natural fit for the site, as well as manufacturing. The practical and majestic ships, primarily lake-going schooners, were the primary means of transporting goods until railways began to replace canal systems all over the state.

Enter the Edisons

The Edison ancestors on his father's side had been mill owners in Holland. Early in the 18th century, they made their way to North America. John Edison (b. 1724), Thomas' great-great-grandfather had come to America as a toddler with his widowed mother. They settled in Caldwell, New Jersey. There were no other children and John's mother never remarried. Little is known of how they fared in his early years, but he inherited his mother's valuable estate when she passed away. John met and married Sarah Odgen in Hanover, New Jersey in 1765, and they settled into a relatively comfortable life of farming in Orange County. In all they had seven children; Samuel, Adonijah, Catherine, Thomas, Mary, Sarah, and Moses. Well-to-do families like the Edisons enjoyed tastefully furnished homes that included indoor cookstoves for heating and cooking, well-made clothes, and a modest selection of consumer goods such as books, linens, mirrors, and porcelain. Clothing styles followed those in Europe, and depending on class included corsets, full skirts, and headscarves for women, and breeches, wigs, and waistcoats for men. Still, life was challenging, and settler families had to work hard to maintain a comfortable, middle-class lifestyle. In addition to running the farm, the Edison's would have had to acquire fuel for heating, cooking, and lighting oil lamps.

Candles were popular for ease of use and were made of beeswax or costly spermaceti (wax drawn from a Sperm Whale). Once the sun had set, 18th-century families faced the increased dangers of the night. Lighting with oil-fed lamps or candles meant that fires were a constant hazard. Families were often limited activities to one room once darkness fell. This place was usually the parlor or the kitchen, both to conserve fuel and temper the risk of fire. Sedentary tasks such as sewing, and reading were typically accomplished by lamplight after dark, and many suffered strained eyesight as a result. Producing heat and light by burning coal, oil, or wax also had the effect of polluting the air, and coating rooms and garments with soot.

By the final decades of the 18th century, coal gas had been introduced to light the outdoors at night, and some homes as well. Prior to the introduction of gas-fueled street lighting, outdoor lanes and walkways were lit by torches affixed to the sides of buildings provided light for lanes and walkways. Seeking to make the night hours more productive and generally safer often required accepting the risk of fire. Indoors, some families would routinely move furnishing to the edges of their rooms to allow for freer movement in the dark, and restrict the use of candles or other open flames. The way people lived and worked was still dictated mainly by the rising and setting of the sun, and it would be a few decades before the introduction of electric lighting would change many fundamentals of life. John Edison was a United Empire Loyalist (often referred to as Tories), loyal to King George III, and a sworn enemy to the American patriots. New Jersey, the only free state in the north, was an unfortunate choice for the Edisons. The location was crisscrossed by armies throughout the war, creating hazardous conditions, and putting a strain on resources for local people. Almost 300 military engagements took place in the New Jersey area, and colonial armies had two winter encampments in New Jersey. There, they took advantage of readily available natural resources: iron ore, food, and salt to support the war.

. When the American Revolution began to impact the safety of his family and properties, John relocated and is believed to have established a bank in New York. In any case, the family fled. Abandoning their substantial farm and home in Caldwell, New Jersey was a risk, but John and Sarah put the safety of their young family first. Later, John Edison, along with his brother-in-law, Isaac Ogden, returned to the New Jersey area to assess the status of their properties and try to salvage whatever resources the armies had missed, but due to bad timing, he was captured and imprisoned for his loyalist sentiments. John and his brother-in-law were chained and held in jail in Morristown for almost a year, and they might have been executed, but Sarah's father, a Colonel in the Continental Army, stepped in and managed to secure a pardon for both men by exchanging them for a British prisoner. Still, they were stripped of their land and given little option but to follow other banished Loyalists to the north. John took his family to Nova Scotia where they were granted 500 acres of farmland in Marshalltown and Digby, but before they left, he wisely deposited a large part of his fortune into an account with the Bank of New England. In Nova Scotia, John farmed and held several positions in government. Thomas' grandfather, Samuel Ogden Edison, was born in Marshalltown in 1804, as one of three sons. In 1811 John and Sarah relocated their family once again, this time to Vienna, in Elgin County, Ontario. By this time Samuel Sr. (Thomas' grandfather) was already married and had eight children, including Edison's father, Samuel Ogden Edison Junior.

Located above the northeastern shore of Lake Erie, Vienna was a mostly unsettled region in 1811, known as the Talbot Settlement. Samuel Sr. built a homestead on the banks of Otter Creek. This was no easy task. The nearest sawmill was 20 miles north, and no roads had been built. The weather made footpaths mostly impassable in winter and spring. Still, the hearty Edisons lived in tents until their log cabins were ready. Samuel Sr. was also a captain in the War of 1812, as much a United Empire Loyalist as his father had been, and sadly part of the losing side of history.

It was in Ontario that Edison's father, an innkeeper, married a schoolteacher, Nancy Elliot, daughter of Ebenezer Matthews Elliot, a Captain in Washington's army, and Mercy Peckham, daughter of a Scottish Quaker. In the years that followed, Canada embraced representative government and Thomas' father, Samuel, was left with two choices – flee to the U.S. or to Bermuda. Bermuda had become a central player in the War after the Union Navy created a blockade to restrict confederate access to southern ports. Ostensibly a British Island, Bermuda was overrun with blockade runners, and unresolved political issues made it too insecure to be truly safe for the Edison familSo, in 1837 Samuel Ogden Edison fled Canada, walked 182 miles to his new home and settled in Milan, Ohio. His wife Nancy, and their three children, Marion, William and Harriet Ann, were left behind and would follow him a few months later. When leaving Canada, they abandoned the flagging Upper Canada Rebellion, where exhausted rebels were losing the battle to British authority in Upper Canada (now Ontario). The Lieutenant Governor, Sir Francis Bond Head, had made insincere gestures to try to appease a restless public, who were pushing back against the authoritarian British style of government. Not above using violence to get his way (he'd employed protestant supporters to 'encourage' electors to cast their votes for him), Bond Head manipulated elections and saw to it that proponents for a responsible (democratic) government were ousted. One of those reformers, William Lyon Mackenzie, threw himself into the fray by launching serialized publications in support of the American Revolution, and calling for immediate changes including separation of church and state, elections for all government positions, freedom of the press, and rights to personal property: all anathema to the wishes of the Crown. The political and economic paradigm was shifting, and loyalists were caught in the powerful wave of change. The rebellion in Upper Canada followed on the heels of a similar, but more successful effort in Lower Canada (Quebec), and history tends to blame Mackenzie for its failure, as he was responsible for enlisting an untrained gang of rebel farmers in a failed march on Toronto. Bond Head rejected the marcher's demands, and although outnumbered, Bond Head's men took the day with their superior weapons and tactical skills.

Now removed from his duty to the King, Samuel held a variety of jobs in Milan, including shingle making in a business deal with his brother, who delivered the bolts to Milan. The shingle business was profitable, and Samuel used his share of earnings to purchase a tavern. He also dabbled in land speculation, although his gambles were seldom successful. Thomas Edison would even have a weakness for speculative investing, and many of his investments also failed, but neither Thomas nor his father stood still long enough to allow any setback to take hold. Optimistic, and always on the lookout for new opportunities, the Edison's were nothing if not resilient. Overall, the Edison family was materially comfortable, and they had some influential friends to help them through some of the more challenging transitions they faced. Captain Alva Bradley, a significant player in the development of the Great Lakes shipping industry, was a family friend, and Thomas' middle name is a result of their acquaintance. Nancy and the children traveled to Milan aboard Captain Bradley's ship *The Indiana.*

Edison's Mother and Life in Port Huron

Nancy Matthews Elliott was born sometime between 1808 and 1810 in New Berlin, New York. Raised in a Scottish Presbyterian household, Nancy attended high school in Canada and placed a high value on education. It's likely Nancy was as much of a supporter of independence for America as her father had been. Presbyterianism is itself a reformist faith system that runs on representative assemblies. A studio portrait of Nancy shows a pale, solemn woman, but she'd been a pretty girl, and it's likely more a reflection of the severe nature of portraiture during that time than a reflection of her personality. In the portrait, Nancy is broad across the face, and her eyes are sunken in shadows. Her hair is neatly tucked into a cloth head covering, and she's dressed in swaths of heavy and pleated taffeta, or perhaps silk. Nancy's family was not wealthy but fit neatly into the upper-middle classes of their hardworking community. When baby Thomas Alva was born on February 11, 1847, Nancy had already lost two infants, and a third died that same year. Such losses were not uncommon at the time, many women gave birth unattended by a physician or midwife, and there were few remedies for infants who became ill. All the same, most parents grieved deeply whenever a child was lost. In 1842, Nancy and

Samuel's son named Carlisle died at age six, and three-year-old Samuel died a year later. Three-year-old Eliza died just months before Thomas was born. Nancy had always been a severe and somewhat reserved woman, though not ungenerous. She was a pious and charitable member of the community and well liked. The Edison home was a site of frequent visits from neighbors, and Nancy was a welcoming hostess. Still, the loss of so many of her children was a massive blow, and Nancy dressed in black for the rest of her life. Marion Edison, Thomas' oldest sister, survived the rigors of infancy and childhood and together with Nancy, fussed over Thomas for much of his infancy and childhood.

There is a much-retold story about Edison's Mother, Nancy. She possessed a formal education (unlike Thomas' father) and believed all her children should be formally educated, preferably outside of the home. Once, young Thomas came home from school with a note from his teacher, Mr. Crawford. Nancy unfolded the paper and read aloud to her son that the schoolteacher found Thomas brilliant, "a genius," and the school had little to offer him and she should teach him herself. Many years later, Edison found the same scrap of paper and read that, in fact, his primary teacher had described him as "addled" and mentally deficient Edison had been expelled, and Nancy had cleverly disguised the harsh reality of the situation. A different version of the famous story relates that the teacher told Edison he was addled, and that the boy, incensed, left school in a huff. The veracity of these stories is questionable, but Nancy *was* a teacher and did teach little Thomas at home. The young scholar had the advantage of an extensive at-home library and a mother's complete devotion to his success. Still, Thomas had done poorly at day school, rejecting the exceedingly dull practice of rote learning, and chafing at the restrictive schedule. In later life, Edison would prove to have a remarkable memory, and the ability to quote extensively from scientific papers, but as a youngster memorization was only a nuisance. He struggled particularly in mathematics, and he irritated his teachers with too many questions. 'Al' as friends and family knew young Thomas, also missed many school days due to sickliness, including a bout of scarlet fever. Regardless of why Thomas' mom took him under her educational wing, it must have had the desired effect. She released him from the strict, structured, and religion-based 'common' schools of the time, and instead encouraged him to pursue his interests. Nancy Edison believed in *life-long learning* before the terminology existed. She encouraged her bright son to explore and engage with everything that interested his young mind. Still, in some respects, Thomas was an immature child. He didn't speak at all until he was almost four years old, and was given to tantrums. Nancy persisted. She gave him books including *School of Natural Philosophy* by R. G. Parker, and later *The Dictionary of Science*. The protégé was hooked, and the science of how things work became Edison's consuming passion. Once, at around age four, he sat on a nest of goose eggs to see if he could hatch them. Nancy encouraged his curiosity, and Thomas asked her, and any other adult around to explain the workings of every object or phenomenon that caught his eye. He wondered how birds balanced on tiny branches, and why bread dough rose in the oven. He liked to wander the town, millworks, rail, and shipyards, intent on learning all he could about the goings on around him. Some may have thought his curiosity a peculiar quality, and it was mainly bothersome to those around him who didn't know the answers to his endless questions. Nancy, though, encouraged his questions and showed him how to discover answers for himself. Edison once remarked, "My mother was the making of me. She understood me; she let me follow my bent. She was so true, so sure of me, and I felt I had someone to live for, someone I must not disappoint."

Edison was not immune to hijinks. In one recollection, young Thomas got the idea that humans should be able to fly. He thought that ingesting a large quantity of effervescent powder – producing its lighter than air bubbles, would make it possible! He talked the Edison's hired boy, Michael Oates, into undertaking the experiment on his behalf. Michael, ever dutiful, ingested the powder and leaped from a tree flapping his arms wildly. When Nancy found out what had happened, Edison got a taste of the willow switch and turned his attention to other interests.

After a quarter-century of steady grain trade, a railroad was established in a nearby town, and the grain-based economy of Milan slipped. At age seven, just as Milan's prosperity began to wane, Thomas and the Edison family moved to Port Huron, Michigan. Samuel took a position with the Fort Gratiot military post as lighthouse keeper and carpenter. After just three months at the local public school, Thomas made his exit from formal education. He'd found trouble outside of school as well: burning a barn to its timbers as an experiment. Thomas always made use of whatever was around him to learn more about the world.

He was known to create mini-laboratories in sheds, barns, or any other space where he could store a few of his experiments. Thomas' somewhat odd appearance also set him apart from his peers. A broad forehead, inherited from his mother's side, and unusually large head may have been the reason his teacher suspected him of mental shortcomings. The so-called science of *phrenology*: the analysis of individual strengths and weaknesses based on the shape and size of the head, gained popularity in North America popular culture early in the 19th century. Little more than a footnote in some historical accounts, phrenology had a widespread impact on medicine, criminology, anthropology, art, education, and literature. It was the impetus for social changes, in part because its philosophy suggested that human traits were innate. The notion that differences in an individual's biological makeup could be responsible for other differences: intelligence, morality, ability, etc., was anathema to the widely accepted religious belief that God created all persons equally, and that it was upbringing that was responsible for deviations. As an adult, Edison once remarked, "I never knew I had an inventive talent until phrenology told me. I was a stranger to myself until then." In fact, Thomas showed signs of unusual intelligence early in life. Once, before even attending primary school, he was spotted in the town, copying the names on shop signs onto a slate. Samuel once said that Thomas "never had any boyhood days; his earliest amusements were steam engines and mechanical forces."

Nancy believed wholeheartedly in her son's abilities, and it was she who is responsible for the young man's confidence and willingness to pursue his sometimes eccentric interests. Still, she wasn't opposed to wielding a willow switch when he disobeyed her: like many other Milan youngsters he occasionally strayed too close to the canal and fell in! Once he slipped into a grain silo and might have suffocated if an older and stronger boy had not rescued him.

Sadly, Nancy struggled with a 'nervous condition,' mental illness in the lingua franca, and died far too young, when Thomas was only 24.

After Nancy's death in 1871, Samuel quickly married again, this time to their former housekeeper: 16-year-old Mary Sharlow. Samuel and Mary had three daughters together, and Samuel lived until 1896. Longevity is a hallmark of the male Edison line and meant Samuel had the opportunity to witness his son's triumphs and even participated in some meaningful ways.

Samuel introduced young Thomas to the philosophies of Thomas Paine. Paine was an enlightenment philosopher and pamphleteer who promoted the idea that science should trump religion in daily affairs. Like Edison, Paine experimented with the invention: designing bridges and doing experiments with gas. Edison became a great admirer of the rationalist philosopher and wrote, "We never had a sounder intelligence in this Republic." Edison, like Paine, developed a great belief in the human capacity for greatness and said, "If we did all the things we are capable of, we would literally astound ourselves." Young Edison was a keen reader, and he would continue the habit, selecting texts from a broad range of interests, throughout his lifetime, but his interest in Paine's ideas endured.

Edison's increasing deafness caused difficulty for the young schoolchild in Port Huron. At age 12, Edison began working for the Grand Trunk Railroad as a candy, magazine and newspaper vendor. Around this same time, Thomas discovered he had a severe hearing loss – perhaps due to his bout of fever. Regardless, the young entrepreneur traveled alone and developed his skills as a salesman. His desire to succeed, and to seek opportunities wouldn't allow for any impediments. This characteristic sustained Edison throughout his career. He was even bold enough to set up a chemistry laboratory for his experiments, and a small, secondhand printing press in one of the baggage cars! Sadly, Thomas' formal education ended early, and by his early teens, Edison was considered functionally deaf.

Edison refused to have surgery for the condition, although it may have helped him. He was afraid if he could hear, he would no longer be able to think. Later it led him to develop the essential carbon transmitter for Bell's telephone because he had difficulty hearing its faint sounds. "The telephone as we now know it might have been delayed," Edison pointed out that "...if a deaf electrician had not undertaken the job of making it a practical thing." As for the phonograph, he explained: "Deafness, pure and simple, was responsible for the experimentation which perfected the machine."

His family had recently relocated to Port Huron, due to increasingly depressed economic conditions in Milan. The town leaders in Milan had made a miscalculation about the importance of railways, and as the canal business faltered, so did the once-prosperous town. Like so many other young men of that era, Edison worked to remove the burden of his care from his family. What set Edison apart was his drive to continue to educate himself long after he had left the classroom. One of his tricks for earning a bit of extra cash was to inflate the price of newspapers on days when there was significant news from the Civil War. He also dabbled in producing his own newspapers using the old printing press and 300lbs of old type he'd purchased from the Detroit Free Press. He named one of his newspapers *The Grand Trunk Herald* and the other (produced with the help of a less experienced hawker) he titled *Paul Pry.* The content of this last publication was objectionable to at least one indignant reader who dunked Thomas in the icy St. Clair River in lieu of canceling a subscription. Still, the publication had several contributing writers and regular subscribers. In the four years he pursued his news career, he earned close to $2,000 and gave most of it to his parents. He never returned to journalism in a serious way, but Edison became a prolific journal writer, producing nearly five million pages of notes and observations in his lifetime, and much of what we know about his life, and his inventions, comes from his words.

Port Huron was not much to Edison's liking, and this was exacerbated when he accidentally set fire to a rail car and was thrown to the hard ground trying to escape the flames. When the angry conductor caught up with him and boxed his ears, Thomas sustained another injury to his already damaged hearing.

The first European to mention Port Huron was Father Louis Hennepin in 1679. Traveling the Great Lakes with Robert de la Salle (1643-1687) aboard a 45-ton barque, Le Griffon, he noted the rich abundance of resources in the area. Located at the mouth of the Black River where it enters the St. Clair River, the area was first explored by Daniel Greysolon Deluth (1636-1710) who established Ft. St. Joseph in 1686. Before that though, Algonquin-speaking tribes of the Great Lakes region had already lived off the bounty of the densely wooded landscape, rich in both flora and fauna. Sadly, the success of European enterprises would mean the end for many of the tribes who once had farmed, fished and traded in the region. The changes coming to the continent were far-reaching and well beyond what could then be imagined. Settlers for a time thought they'd won the west but were in for a sea change in all aspects of their societies. For Thomas, the ability to transmit information instantly via telegraph was the most significant of those changes and launched him from early entrepreneurial efforts into a life-changing obsession with inventing and improving upon technology.

Telegraphy and Leaving Home

By age 14, Thomas was comfortable in the railway world. Once, as he and a young companion kicked rocks along the tracks in Port Huron, Michigan, Thomas noticed a toddler messing about on the tracks ahead, unmindful of rolling boxcar. Edison sprang into action and whisked the boy away just in time. The boy's father was J.U. MacKenzie, a stationmaster in neighboring Mount Clemens, Michigan. He described the events saying, "My son, then two and a half years old, unobserved by his nurse had strayed upon the main track and was amusing himself throwing pebbles, when Edison, who stood near with papers under his arm, turned and saw the child's danger. Throwing aside his papers, he plunged between the cars just in time to drag himself and the child clear of the approaching cars." MacKenzie was grateful for Edison's quick-thinking bravery, and he offered to train Thomas to become a telegrapher as a reward for his courage and presence of mind. The profession of telegraphy, though popular, had a less-than-lily-white reputation. Unsavory activities like drinking and gambling were pervasive, perhaps because it was largely a young man's game and involved late hours and long shifts of work. Often, Edison was cold and hungry. Edison's problems weren't linked to vice, however; he was let go from numerous telegrapher positions for sending messages and conducting 'experiments' without authorization. Sometimes he'd be homeless between telegraphy jobs. Always the maverick, Edison was unconcerned and soon began devising ways to improve the existing telegraphic system. In 1864, he came up with the idea that reduced errors in telegraphed messages. Called a *Morse Repeater*, the invention slowed down the message at the receiving end by punching the dots and dashes of Morse code into a slower running strip of paper, resulting in fewer operator errors.

This work carried Edison into maturity and established his reputation for inventiveness. In 1866, at age 19, Edison relocated to Louisville, a busy place that year given it was the location for Union soldiers to muster and finally be released to their homes following the end of the war. Kentucky had declared an end to the war, and the streets filled with celebrants: freed slaves and soldiers alike. The Western Union hired Edison to work the Associated Press bureau news wire. Edison preferred working nights so that he might read and experiment in peace. In fact, he spent so much time alone in his room working on inventions and improvements that some of his co-workers referred to him as 'the Looney.' Edison was unmoved. He had found his calling in scientific and technological experimentation, and he was unapologetic! It was during this time that Edison developed his unusual sleeping routine. He never slept more than three or four hours at a spell, and often stated he felt sleep constituted a waste of his time. He felt any state that diminished productivity must be banished, and he later chose employees based on their physical stamina, and ability to concentrate late into the night saying, "At first the boys had some difficulty in keeping awake, and would go to sleep under stairways and in corners... We employed watchers to bring them out, and in time they got used to it."

Two years later, Edison moved to Boston where, still with the Western Union, he continued to experiment and invent. He had a knack for quick comprehension of mechanical devices, and as his confidence grew, he decided to resign. In 1869, Edison was determined to invent full time and make his fortune. The relationship between Edison's innovations and to the acquisition of wealth was unequivocal. He once remarked, "Anything that won't sell I don't want to invent. Sales are proof of utility and utility is success."

He began this new phase with an invention that recorded legislative votes. It was a failure, although a fellow telegrapher, DeWitt Roberts, invested the exorbitant sum of $100 in the concept. When Edison demonstrated the invention for a congressional committee, they flatly rejected it as anathema to the intentionally slow system for gathering votes already in place. Now out of funds, and discouraged, Edison made a move to the growing metropolis of New York. There, telegraph engineer Franklin L. Pope befriended Edison. He saw his potential and offered him a place to sleep: at the offices of the New York Gold Indicator Company.

Luckily, Edison was on site when the master ticker tape machine broke down and was able to repair it. He was promptly offered a job. Later that same year he refashioned the invention for use in the stock exchange, and his Universal Stock Ticker made him a small fortune. By connecting the central office of Western Union with outlying stations, Thomas created a network of communications that was precedent setting. His adaptations made it possible to transmit four messages at a time over a single wire. He asked the Western Union to pay $5,000 for the invention and was more than a little surprised when they paid him $30,000 instead.

With the windfall in hand, Edison invested in a Newark, New Jersey telegraph machine factory. The factory became Edison's first 'official' inventing workshop: Menlo Park.

Inventing the Future in Menlo Park

It is said Edison chose the Menlo Park site because it was the highest point along the Pennsylvania Railroad between New York and Philadelphia. The new laboratory in West Orange, New Jersey was much more than just a building, or business. Edison had clear goals, and a vision of a space where he would have ready access to tools, equipment, artifacts, chemicals, and supplies to achieve them. His stated wish was to produce "a minor invention every 10 days, and a big thing every six months or so." He wanted to have whatever he required to create, test, and demonstrate his inventions on hand. Recently widowed, Samuel Edison was at his ambitious son's side to oversee the development of the property, and ensure it met Thomas' exacting standards. He was also there to keep an eye on the bookkeeping, as Thomas was known to spend freely, and even to give money away without a thought for the longer term. The original laboratory was a nondescript, white building that might easily have been mistaken for a church hall. To Edison, it was his *Invention Factory*, and inside he lined the walls with intricate shelving, and set out large worktables in an open plan to allow for ease of movement between projects and to encourage collaboration among his assistants. Edison liked to jump from one project to another, flitting about his workshop as inspiration dictated. It was a lighthearted workplace, despite long hours, and there were often pranks and friendly jokes between Edison and his assistants. In addition to the laboratory building, Edison built a carpentry shop, a blacksmith's shop, a glass house and a carbon shed. This last was a small wooden hut that held dozens of kerosene lamps. The lamps were kept lit, monitored, and soot they produced was collected for use in transmitters, as well as in other Edison experiments.

Menlo Park was the site of some of Edison's most important and prescient successes. Fifteen years prior to British physicist J. J. Thompson's discovery of electrons, one of Edison's engineers, William J. Hammer, "noted a blue glow around the positive pole in a vacuum bulb and a blackening of the wire and the bulb at the negative pole." This phenomenon was caused by thermionic emissions from electrons and resulted in the development of an electron tube, critical to the electronics industry that followed.

The Menlo Park property, 34 acres, was purchased from the family of William Carman, and Edison chose the office of the former Menlo Park real estate development company, Menlo Park Land Company, to be his home.

One reporter describes the three-story frame house as "without a trace of ostentation," but was, in fact, a model of nineteenth-century bourgeoisie living complete with a formal library, bronze statuary, and a piano-forte. The Edison's had three servants to help with household chores and with the children, and Mary's sister Alice also lived in the Menlo Park home. Edison said of their new home "I like it first-rate out here in the green country and can study, work, and think." Mary though was less enamored of their new country lifestyle and slept with a pistol nearby. She was often vexed when Thomas did not come home from work until "early morning, and sometimes not at all."

Other Menlo Park staff built homes on the property, and a small community was formed. For unmarried staff, a boardinghouse run by an Edison relative, Mrs. Sarah Jordan, provided a cozy bed and home-cooked meals. This arrangement suited Edison well, as he liked to keep his staff working late, and have them on hand should he need their help.

Edison initially took on two assistants, John Kreusi: a machinist born in 1843 in Switzerland, and Charles Batchelor: a draughtsman and mechanist born in 1845 in Great Britain. They worked on numerous projects together. Soon after, Edison hired his soon-to-be wife, Mary Stilwell. Born in Newark in 1855.

Mary was only 16 when Edison noticed her. The best-known photo of her shows a dark-haired beauty, with excellent features: soft, clear eyes, a tiny waist, and a tumble of heat-set curls falling on her shoulder. They married on Christmas day in 1871. Mary was frail and anxious; perhaps due to her young age and was not well equipped for the rigors of life married to a man like Edison, who was distracted and focused almost entirely on his work. Like many women of that era, Mary was likely prescribed a course of opiate-based medication by their family physician. Complaints both physical and mental were routinely treated with doses of morphine-laced drugs during the era, and there was little understanding of the potential for dependency. Women who struggled with mental health were considered 'hysterics' and treated with medicine to calm and soothe them. It is believed Mary's death may have been caused by an overdose of an opiate. It is not difficult to imagine Mary, a lonely and overburdened teenager seeking solace in a soothing elixir of morphine. Edison was less than thrilled with Mary's intellect or inventing abilities and kept a journal on the subject. He wrote: "Mrs. Mary Edison My Wife Dearly Beloved Cannot invent worth a Damn!!"

Mary and Thomas had three children. Marion Estelle Edison was born in 1873, Thomas Alva Edison Jr. in 1876, and William Leslie Edison in 1878. All three children were under the age of ten when they lost their mother. Edison charmingly nicknamed his older children 'Dot' and 'Dash' for the now widely used telegraphic code words. However, he was a distant parent, preferring his inventing lab to home and hearth. The children were cared for by servants and extended family and sent to various boarding schools as soon as they were old enough to attend. Also during this period, his electrical lighting system was losing business, and Edison was in financial distress. He even had to borrow $500 to give his wife a proper burial.

Around the time of Mary's death, Edison was distracted by the work of Alexander Graham Bell, whose *telephone* was turning heads around the world. The Western Union sought Edison's expertise in developing the newfangled telephone for practical purposes. Bell's work, though impressive by any standard, was not without flaws. Most significantly, due to the type of transmitter he built, the range of transmission was limited. The strength of the current needed to be increased. Drawing from his understanding of developments in British cable telegraph, Edison began to experiment with carbon for resistance. His improvements established the basic technology that would be used in telephone communication until the digital technology became standardized in the 1980s. The patent for Edison's transmitter was filed April 27, 1877, two weeks after another ingenious inventor, Emile Berliner, had submitted his claim to the concept. It would take decades for the matter to be resolved. Eventually, Berliner's patent was deemed invalid in favor of Edison's. Numerous hearings and dozens of lawsuits were launched in the years that followed. Western Union, Edison, Bell and other vital players wrangled with each other for years in the attempt to hold ownership of telephone technology, and eventually, Bell would become the world leader in telecommunications. There are a few pertinent speculations about how the relationship between Bell and Edison may have been impacted by their differing attitudes towards deafness. Bell believed developing a functional hearing aid was the best possible option for deaf patients (although he never developed one himself). Edison, on the other hand, was repelled by the thought of an invention to improve hearing. It is possible he did not want to draw attention to his deafness. This refusal to invent something to help his hearing is supported by the fact he used Morse code by tapping, particularly in communications with his family members, rather than sign language. Conversely, Edison once commented his ability to concentrate and think deeply was in part due to his deafness. Completely deaf in one ear, and close to 80% deaf in the other, Thomas once said he'd last heard a bird sing at age 12. Bell firmly believed that vocalization (then called *oralism*) was a superior form of communication, and he promoted speech even for the profoundly deaf. He also believed that *manualism*, or the uses of sign language, facilitated the intermarriage of deaf people, and thus create a 'defective race' of the deaf. He recommended that parents sterilize their deaf children. Edison did not share this eugenicist.

The Industrial Revolution and Lighting New York

The speed of social and economic change that took place during the 19th century left many individuals and societies reeling. The vast scale of expansion in industry, transport, international trade, and consumption of goods was unprecedented, and the impact of many of the changes was profound and irreversible. Contemporary societies have grown accustomed to rapid developments in technology, and the regular appearance and availability of new products.

This was not the case prior to the Victorian era. Inventions that shaped the century included the steam engine, which James Watt adapted from steam-powered water extraction used in mining for use in steam trains. The new trains had an unprecedented impact on the transportation of people and goods. Faster and safer than travel by horse, or horse and carriage, steam trains could also travel much greater distances and were less likely to be robbed (though not altogether inviolable). The transit of people by steam train is in large part responsible for the settlement of remote parts of the Americas, but also for access to larger markets. Settlers could access necessary good and tools within a reasonable distance, and they could get their own resources and products to distant markets.

Another famous invention, the spinning jenny, commenced a wave of invention that reduced the need for labour through mechanization of processes such as weaving cloth.

The spinning jenny used eight spindles to spin eight threads with a single wheel. Prior to its invention, cloth had been made at a much slower pace using the spinning wheel. Textiles became the first truly *industrialized* industry because of the spinning jenny and other inventions that followed including the cotton gin and the water frame.

Other inventions also contributed to the rapid shifts underway in society. In 1810, a British merchant, Peter Durand, patented the tin can. Before him, the Government of France offered a prize to anyone who could come up with a new way to preserve food for Napoleon Bonaparte's military forces, and Nicolas Appert received the prize when he invented the process of sterilization using pressurized glass containers. Durand adapted Appert's technique to a tin plate container which was cheaper to produce and less likely to burst under pressure. The new method for preserving food was not without opponents, and many unfortunate incidents involving tainted preserving processes almost scuttled the invention altogether. One businessman, John Gamble, was found to have shipped contaminated canned meat to the British Navy, and it's long been believed the unfortunates of the Franklin Expedition also succumbed to poorly sealed tinned meat. Eventually, though, canned food became a staple of the western diet, and changed agriculture from a seasonal industry to a year-round, multi-million-dollar concern.

Not all the impacts of the Industrial Revolution were as positive. Cities became overcrowded as more rural people sought factory and millwork.

The success of some aspects of industrial enterprise resulted in crowded housing conditions, poor sanitation, increased air pollution from concentrated levels of coal and wood-burning, and many other increased threats to health.

With concentrated population, crime increased as well, and instead of creating considerable wealth and prosperity for all, the industrial revolution added to the stratification of society.

The promise of real financial and social success was only attainable by a very lucky, or clever few. Much of society stepped onto a treadmill of labour that has persisted until this day.

For all the noble motivations behind 18th and 19th-century innovations, the desire to amass capital, and access ever-larger markets also had a significant influence.

Thomas Edison had a knack for capitalizing on his own inventions, as well as those of others. As he honed his skills and processes, he'd become addicted to the feeling and wages of success. His work on a new and improved light bulb is a prime example of how he combined ingenuity with savvy business sense.

Edison's light bulb was not the first, but it was the first practical and commercially realistic version of the new technology. Like much of Edison's work, he and his team excelled at modifying and improving existing inventions to meet market and manufacturing demands. In 1802, Humphry Davy, an accomplished chemist from Cornwall, England created the first incandescent light, using a platinum strip as the conductor. Others followed in his footsteps, tweaking the materials and design of the bulb along the way. Edison, for his part, made two significant improvements on previous light bulb prototypes. Firstly, he had implemented a filament that was both economical and long-lasting. Made from carbonized sewing thread, and then later, from bamboo fibers, it was a perfect solution to an old problem – how to heat something to a high enough degree to emit light, but not to burn. The notion of using bamboo for the filament may have come from a camping trip when Edison is reported to have dropped a bamboo fishing-pole into a campfire and noticed its unusual burning properties. Secondly, he created a technique for evacuating the bulb of oxygen using the Sprengel Pump. Invented in England in 1865, the Sprengel Pump used mercury drops to compress and remove air from a tube and served Edison's purposes perfectly. It was no straightforward project to come to the right combination of technologies. In Edison's own words: "I speak without exaggeration when I say that I have constructed three thousand different theories in connection with the electric light, each one of them reasonable and appears to be true. Yet only in two cases did my experiments prove the truth of my theory. My chief difficulty, as perhaps you know, was in constructing the carbon filament, the incandescence of which is the source of the light. Every quarter of the globe was ransacked by my agents, and all sorts of the queerest materials were used until finally the shred of bamboo now utilized was settled upon. Even now, I am still at work nearly every day on the lamp, and quite lately I have devised a method of supplying sufficient current to fifteen lamps with one horsepower. Formerly ten lamps per horse-power was the extreme limit."

He created a bulb that burned for days at a time, used it to light his home, his street, and eventually, the world. Edison knew perfecting the bulb would only solve part of the problem of electric lighting. Friend and physicist George Barker invited Edison to visit and observe an arc light system that had been developed in Connecticut, and Edison was enthralled. Newly inspired, he drew up plans for a multi-channel distribution of electricity using 15 or 20 of the dynamos he'd witnessed in operation at Barker's, and a 500-horsepower engine. His vision combined his understanding of how gas was distributed at the time, and how telegraphs signals traveled. His challenge was to devise ways to regulate and divide current across multiple channels. He developed lamp regulators, to prevent the incandescent materials from melting, and once that problem was solved, he had to come up with a way to allow for control of individual lamps. Placing lamps along a parallel circuit (as opposed to a series circuit), made it possible to operate lamps independently.

The demand for his invention was overwhelming, and in response, Edison built the first light bulb factory in an old wooden building close to the Menlo Park facility. The Edison Electric Light Company, established in 1878, also became the home base for several other experimental projects. Edison ran the first electric train from his machine shop at the west end of Menlo Park; to his copper mine a few blocks away. Consisting of only three small rail cars, Edison continued to develop the line until it was operating both passenger and freight service.

Edison tested the efficacy of his bulbs in individual businesses like Hinds, Ketcham & Company, a printing company in New York City. However, this process of installing a dynamo for each separate building was costly. A centralized power station would solve the problem, so Edison tested the concept in the United Kingdom at the Holborn Viaduct in London. After a successful two-year pilot, Edison was ready to transfer his success to America. In 1882, Edison built a generating plant in the center of New York City on Pearl Street. Edison intentionally selected a well-populated part of the city and one that boasted both commercial and residential activities. The Pearl Street area, also known as the First District, was located between Wall Street, Nassau Street, the East River, and Spruce Street.

At the time, this area was considered the financial hub of North America, if not the world. Also, major newspapers including the *New York Times* were headquartered in the First District, a promotional advantage that did not escape Edison's keen business acumen. He purchased two Pearl Street buildings to house his generator and had the floors reinforced to handle the extra weight of machinery – which he called 'Jumbo' named for PT Barnum's famous elephant. In all, six dynamos, driven by reciprocating steam engines, were required to accomplish the task of distributing electricity throughout the district. In fact, the technical requirements were vast and included underground installation of 80,000 feet of conductors, a job that employed many hands. Once everything was in place, Edison and his investors met with Chief Electrician John W. Lieb at the Drexel, Morgan and Company offices to flip the switch closed. On that first day, 400 lamps were simultaneously lit and were soon to be followed by thousands more. The New York

Times reported the event under its 'Miscellaneous News' section, somewhat underestimating the impact of the momentous occasion.

The success of this event made Edison a household name. It also made him a very wealthy man. Now investors regularly visited Menlo Park, alongside tourists, and Edison used their money to design and patent hundreds and eventually thousands of new inventions. Despite his success, some in the scientific community derided Edison as a re-fashioner of the ideas of others. There was some truth to the accusation, for although Edison had his own approach to scientific discovery, he also took any opportunity that presented itself to develop or improve on a new idea. Edison had a pragmatic streak that served him well.

The Phonograph and Moving Pictures

By the time of his success on Manhattan Island, Edison was already developing a fantastic new machine. Intended to transfer telegraphic messages through puncturing paper tape, and later relayed by telegraph, the concept led Edison to wonder if a telephone message could be recorded. It's difficult to say how Edison's loss of hearing as a child may have influenced his work on recording the human voice, but perhaps he wanted to accommodate his sensory disability in some way. He did not conceive the phonograph as an invention to be used for entertainment, and later this would spell the end of the phonograph in favor of 'records' featuring popular songs, speeches, and comic entertainments. Edison's ideas for how the phonograph might be used are surprising. In June 1878, he described for the North American Review how it could be employed in dictation and letter writing, recording books and other educational materials, and even to create a record of the voice of a dying family member.

Edison's phonograph first emerged from his work at Menlo Park in 1877. The first phonograph was a basic device: a pin that pierced paper as it wound around a wooden tube, and a diaphragm that converted vibrations to sound built from Edison's drawings by his colleague, John Kruesi. Edison spoke into the mouthpiece: "Mary had a little lamb," and miraculously the machine repeated his words. Later he would change the tube to waxed paper, and then metal. It was the only invention of its type in the world. The phonograph made Edison a household name. The papers referred to him as "The Wizard of Menlo Park," and excited visitors began flocking to the laboratory to see the miracle at first hand. Edison had to expand his laboratories, and added a machine shop and a library. He preferred the term 'Invention Factory' to describe his growing enterprise. Edison enjoyed the initial rush of fame, attending parties to show off the invention, but the change in his circumstances did not seem to affect his dedication to work. He would often leave soirees thrown in his honor to return to his lab and work on into the night. Soon, his work would pay off in a way even more significant than his imaginings.

In 1877, *Scientific American* reported, "Mr. Thomas A. Edison recently came into this office, placed a little machine on our desk, turned a crank, and the machine inquired as to our health, asked how we liked the phonograph, informed us that it was very well, and bid us a cordial good night." Soon, other newspaper and popular magazines also reported on the invention.

On January 24, 1878, The Edison Speaking Phonograph Company was established to exhibit and sell the invention. Early models were not easy to operate, and wore out quickly, but were still an overnight success.

Edison briefly lost interest in the phonograph, distracted by his interest in electric lighting, and gave his attention to other projects.

Alexander Graham Bell picked up where Edison left off and worked on the phonograph, substituting wax for tin foil and developing a floating stylus to replace the rigid needle. Bell took out a patent and presented his *graphophone* to the public. He asked Edison to work with his collaboration on the machine, but Edison declined. Eventually, Jesse H. Lippincott, a wealthy businessman, took over control of both Bell and Edison's manufacturing concerns and created the American Graphophone Company, later to be renamed the North American Phonograph Company, whose primary business was in renting the machines for special events and office applications. Edison wasn't done with the work yet and began to produce machines for entertainment (including, at one point, talking dolls). His cylinders play music and recitations by famous entertainers and presenters. Edison had lost the rights to his invention, and to get them back was forced to declare bankruptcy. Once his legal issues were settled, Edison returned to the task of selling phonographs, and he established The National Phonograph Company in 1896 to manufacture phonographs. These machines, intended solely for home entertainment, soon expanded his reach to commercial uses both in America and in Europe. Although prices for home-use phonographs had fallen significantly, many thousands of machines were sold featuring a variety of 'entertainments' such as hymns, comedy, ballads, and marches. All this was accomplished without an effective system for mass production, and relied on performers willingness to repeat their performances multiple times! In 1901, a new production method was introduced. It involved molding, rather than engraving the cylinders. Using the new process, Edison's factories could produce up to 150 cylinders per day and used black wax. These cylindrical 'records' sold for 34 cents each. Edison was also producing business machines but had trouble competing with the cheap and popular Columbia Dictaphones already widely in use. By 1916 Edison's *Epiphone* began to grow in popularity.

Inspired by the simulated animal footage created by Eadweard Muybridge's *zoopraxiscope*, Edison's first foray into moving pictures resulted in a rather rough version of what would later become one of his most important inventions. Edison's cylinder with images lined up in order had to be viewed by one individual at a time with a microscope and produced only a hint of what cinema would become, but it was enough of a hint to capture the imagination. His notion was to create an effect that would stimulate the eye in the same way his phonograph appealed to the ear. W.L. Dickson was a member of Edison's staff and a photographer. In 1892, the two men invented a camera called the *Kinetoscope*. They were first shown publicly in 1894 on Broadway, New York in the Holland Brothers Arcade, and the following year the first Edison films were exhibited commercially in 'nickelodeons,' both in America and overseas. Edison's failure to properly patent his technology in Europe allowed French manufacturers Lois and Auguste Lumiere to produce a portable version of the 'peephole' machine, and later a projector version, permitting more than one audience member to view films at a time. They are most famous for their film *Arrival of a Train* which frightened first-time cinemagoers into thinking they were about to be run down.

Edison's movie studio, named "The Black Maria" due to its uncanny resemblance to police paddy wagons, was housed at West Orange, the first of Edison's laboratories, and the tarpaper shack produced close to 75, 20-second films. Ingeniously designed, the roof of Black Maria could be raised, allowing in sunlight. For subject matter, Edison drew upon the traditions of stage and vaudeville and featured dancers, magicians, boxers, and other forms of light entertainment. Edison loved to apply popular fictions to film, and 'stars' like Buffalo Bill and other well-known entertainers of the late 19th and early 20th century went to his studio to commit their likenesses to his unique process. He also specialized in mini-travelogues and had a team travel widely capturing exotic locations and cultures.

Edison's participation in the film industry was contentious. He held so many patents on technology he had control over the industry of film producing, at least briefly. He established the Motion Picture Patent Company, forcing other inventors to work under his leadership. Members of his monopoly only worked with and sold to other members. Eventually, a small group of independent filmmakers decided to leave Edison and his cronies to their devices and relocated to California.

Eventually, film required better projector technology to be commercially successful, and Edison withdrew from the industry as other inventors made headway. The best known of these was Edwin S. Porter and his 1903 film *The Great Train Robbery*.

The World Columbian Exposition

The World Columbian Exposition in Chicago, ostensibly organized to celebrate the 'discovery' of America by Christopher Columbus, was a civic and political response to a series of demoralizing events. The end of the Civil War, while a relief in some senses, also resulted in the mass movement of workers from rural to urban settings. In Chicago, job seekers had to compete with newly mechanized factories, leaving many young men and women far from home and without occupation. Also, an upswell in immigration filled the windy Chicago streets with hopeful immigrants, many from Europe, but also from Asia, South America, and the Caribbean. Some met with resentment and discrimination, and the disparate groups formed insular communities and neighborhoods in response. Black communities experienced forced segregation and a heightened policing of activities, but most other communities self-segregated resulting in enclaves of often disgruntled and unemployed people. The ethnic centers of Chicago provided a feeling of security for the newly arrived, but could also stir xenophobic and racist sentiments. Civic leaders were desperate to create a positive, upbeat reputation for the growing city and they looked to Europe for inspiration.

Expositions in London (1851), and France (1854) had set the bar high. London's offering included an emphasis on developments in automation and manufacturing and showcased the infamous Crystal Palace. Designed by Sir Joseph Paxton, the glass and cast-iron showpiece housed London's 14,000 exhibitors in a building three times the size of St. Paul's Cathedral. The 990,000-square foot wonder was a sensation. The 1854 exposition in Paris also emphasized industry, and agricultural invention. Edison was invited to display in Paris, and upon his return home, he described the exposition in glowing terms, "The Paris Exposition is simply bewildering. It is grand! Immense! If the Americans hope to surpass it, they will have to get to work and never loiter." In 1893, Edison formed a sister company to General Electric in Paris, the Compagnie Francaise Thomson-Houston.

The investors and politicians behind Chicago's effort knew they had to make the fair, not only memorable but also astonishing if they hoped to join the ranks of their predecessors. They sought to amaze visitors with technical and scientific marvels and exhibits from 'exotic' cultures. The Paris fair impressed architects with their centerpiece: The Eiffel Tower, but Chicago would provide both artistic vision and good old-fashioned fun when they unveiled the *Ferris Wheel* as the featured structure of the exhibit. Invented by George Washington Ferris, the one built for Chicago was the first of its kind and more than a million-people paid 50 cents to experience the thrill of riding on a wheel 140 feet into the air. For Americans, it was time to show the world the new kid on the block was ready to play.

In 1893, financial markets in the U.S. collapsed. It was the beginning of a depression that would result in massive unemployment, and in Chicago, banks and well-established companies were forced to close their doors. Workers and the unemployed clashed, and soup kitchens and tenement housing had more mouths to feed and bodies to house than they could handle. This was exacerbated by the evident and extravagant lifestyles of America's top tier.

In 1871, the Chicago's town center had been almost wiped out by a horrific fire. By 1890, the city had largely rebuilt and had become more important commercially than ever before. Accordingly, the planners of the fair sought to make it bigger and more impressive than any other fair. They accomplished their goal with astounding exhibits of arts and manufacturing beyond imagination. Had Edison been more willing to accept advice from his contemporary, Nikola Tesla, the task of powering and lighting the fair might have fallen to his General Electric Company. Thousands of lights were required, and electricity on a scale previously unknown. Sadly, Edison's proposal to power the fair with direct current at the cost of close to half a million dollars was rejected in favor of Westinghouse and Tesla's cheaper bid that proposed alternating current. Edison was not rejected altogether though and "as a tribute to Edison a Tower of Light, a replica of the German Tower of Victory, was placed in the middle of the Electricity Building. The 82-foot tower was topped by a single incandescent bulb 8 feet tall." The 'City of Light' as the fair came to be called, was no disappointment, except perhaps to Edison who garnered little credit for the impact of more than ten thousand incandescent bulbs.

Fair organizers permitted Edison to exhibit phonograph technology within the Electricity Building, and both Edison and his chief competitor, inventor of the *graphophone* Edward Easton, featured and profited from nickel-in-the-slot phonographs placed throughout the exhibition site. One visitor to the fair, Thomas Lambert, was inspired to improve the design for records by his visit to Chicago.

Leading up to the exposition, Edison had other projects in the works. One of these was his Ogdensburg, New Jersey mining concern. Edison believed he had discovered a method to simplify separating iron from rocks. In 1881, Edison incorporated his Edison Ore-Milling Company as a response to his observation of scarcity of iron ore on the eastern seaboard. Edison believed that electromagnetism could draw ore from rock, debris, and even sand, at a fraction of the cost of other processes. He met with numerous failures and technical challenges, closed up shops and opened new ones, lost money and invested more money, all the while believing, unequivocally, in his idea. "I'm going to do something now so different and so much bigger than anything I've ever done before people will forget that my name ever was connected with anything electrical." In 1899, Edison finally accepted that his process, and foray into mining, had failed. However, ever the optimist, Edison parlayed the waste product of his mining business, namely sand, into a cement production project, selling of the material to cement companies, and starting his own: the Edison Portland Cement Company, who eventually bought Edison's improved sand-processing kiln. Yankee Stadium was erected in 1923 using Edison's Portland cement.

Edison, never one to overlook an opportunity, was also a keen early-adopter of automobiles. He enjoyed taking his family for motoring excursions and thinking about ways to improve the battery life of electric cars. His friendship with Henry Ford would get in the way of following through with this project. Henry Ford's Ford Motor Co. (1903) was a customer of Edison's nickel-iron batteries. Although Edison is often credited with pushing Ford to mass-produce his gasoline-driven cars, in fact, Edison realized early-on that electric vehicles were better from almost every angle: "Electricity is the thing. There are no whirring and grinding gears with their numerous levers to confuse. There is not that almost terrifying uncertain throb and whirr of the powerful combustion engine. There is no water-circulating system to get out of order – no dangerous and evil-smelling gasoline and no noise."

Ford was already on the gasoline bandwagon, and money began pouring in, so even though he respected his good friend's opinion, the horse, so to speak, was out of the barn. By 1914, once the auto industry was well and truly Ford's, he did consider an electric model again. The New York Times interviewed Ford who said, "Within a year, I hope, we shall begin the manufacture of an electric automobile. I don't like to talk about things that are a year ahead, but I am willing to tell you something of my plans. The fact is that Mr. Edison and I have been working for some years on an electric automobile that would be cheap and practicable. Cars have been built for experimental purposes, and we are satisfied now that the way is clear to success. The problem so far has been to build a low weight storage battery that would operate for long distances without recharging. Mr. Edison has been experimenting with such a battery for some time." Photos exist of these early experiments – battery operated cars on Model T frames, for the most part, called the 'Edison Ford.' Rumors swirled that the first commercially available Edison-Ford would be on the market in 1915 at the cost of $500-700. Early press said the vehicle could travel as much as 100 miles on a single charge. Some conspiracy theorists suggest the plans for electric vehicles were undermined by oil cartels, which may have set fire to Edison's workshop in 1914. However, it is more likely the car failed because Henry Ford insisted on using Edison's batteries. In fact, Ford purchased 100,000 of the batteries before it was determined they were unsuitable for the purpose. Ford lost close to 1.5 million dollars on the venture, but he and Edison remained friends.

The War of the Currents

The circle of leading inventors and scientists in the field of electricity grew as the 19th century progressed. It was a century of experimentation and advancement in all areas, but technology and mechanical developments outpaced all others. Men such as George Westinghouse and Nikola Tesla would challenge Edison's position as the most significant inventor of all time, and change the nature of how humans live.

George Westinghouse was born in 1846 in Central Bridge: a small hamlet in Albany County located southwest of the better-known town of Schenectady, New York. The family was of German origin, and the name Westinghouse likely changed from *Westinghaus* at some point in the transition from old world to new. His father, George Westinghouse, Sr., was a toolmaker and owned a machine shop where his son conducted early experiments and became enthralled with the potential for steam power. His mother, Emmeline Westinghouse nee Vedder, was Dutch-English and bore eight children during her lifetime, of which George Jr. was the third.

It's likely young George would have pursued a career focused on steam-driven engines, if not for the eruption of the Civil War. George enlisted in 1863 and served in the regiment of the New York cavalry. In 1864, George's younger brother, Albert, was killed in battle. Shortly after, George transferred and was offered a naval commission aboard the U.S.S. Muscoota. The ship soon played an essential role in blocking Jefferson Davis as he attempted to escape Key West. George was ready to return home, and resume his work in his father's shop.

Westinghouse, like Edison, was interested in many avenues of invention. After the war, he made critical improvements to railway travel, most notably in developing reliable braking systems. He also produced improved methods for piping natural gas. The work that put him in conflict with Edison was his promotion of the A/C system for electrical transmission. The infamous "War of Currents," also called the Battle of the Currents, began when both Edison and Westinghouse hoped their preferred system for electrical transmission would win the day. Westinghouse had the expertise of the Serbian electrical genius, Nikola Tesla, to help him affect the changes that A/C required to make it successful. Born in 1856 in Croatia, Tesla was a talented engineer and physicist who impressed the scientific world with his invention of the electromagnetic induction motor.

In 1882, Edison hired Nikola Tesla upon the recommendation of his colleague, Charles Batchelor, a former Edison Continental Company employee. Tesla was excited to be working with the famous genius and hoped to convince him to recognize the superiority of Alternating Current for transmitting electricity. Edison wasn't interested. He'd invested mightily in promoting D/C and tried to cast a shadow over the A/C system, highlighting its potential for danger to human life.

The War of the Currents would wind up in courts of law, and in newspaper headlines, pitting the two renaissance men against each other. Edison sued Westinghouse multiple times for infringing on his patents. Edison also attempted to halt the success of the A/C system by lobbying senators to restrict allowable voltages. Both sides had victories and losses, but in 1893 Westinghouse, along with Tesla, won the right to provide electric light for the Chicago World's

Columbian Exposition. He took another victory when he beat out numerous competitors for the rights to develop the electrical potential of the Niagara Escarpment.

Edison's 1879 incandescent light bulb was powered by D/C current, and the potential for cashing in on the rapid development of D/C hydroelectric plants was hard for him to resist. Still, Edison knew the D/C system was flawed. It simply was unable to manage the distances, and the variability required to truly power up the nation. He too sought the expertise of Nikola Tesla to improve D/C, but the Serbian genius had terrible news – it couldn't be done. Although Tesla possessed mathematical knowledge, and had developed many other improvements to electrical transmission and devices, Edison was dismissive of Tesla's conclusion. It wasn't what Edison wanted to hear, and he stiffed Tesla on the deal, paying him a mere fraction of what he'd been promised.

Bravado aside, Edison knew Westinghouse and A/C had a leg up. The A/C system was making inroads into both urban and rural markets. Edison, an avowed anti-death penalty supporter, decided to publicly challenge A/C because he believed it was both deadly and inhumane to apply it to humans *or* animals, and to beat Westinghouse at his own game. He gave public demonstrations, using live subjects including small dogs, in which the poor animal was lured into shocking itself to death. The circus sideshow aspect of Edison's business was not unique during the 19th century – or indeed to Edison, who'd largely cashed in on the phonograph with a Barnum and Bailey-like approach to marketing. Many inventors followed suit. Tesla was renowned for demonstrating his electric coils by summoning what appeared to the 19th-century audience as room-sized lightening!

The main flaw in the DC system was its limitation in terms of distance of transmission (about ¼ mile). This was not so much an issue in urban centers, where one dynamo or generator could provide electricity to service to multiple homes or offices within a single building. Edison knew perfectly well the Niagara project was well beyond what DC could handle, but he kept his hat in the ring regardless.

Alternating Current was also an imperfect system. For one thing, the motor Westinghouse employed was inefficient and unwieldy. Tesla worked on it feverishly, but could not complete the work at a pace that satisfied Westinghouse. Edison's DC stations numbered around 1,500, spread across factories and other commercial interests, and primarily powered lighting systems, although Direct Current had been implemented for other purposes as well. One of the reasons why Edison's systems garnered lesser success than Alternating Current, may have been that Edison had very little interest in motors, or in providing electrical power to industry for that matter, and outsourced the building of his motors to the Sprague Electric Railway and Motor Company.

Danish physicist and chemist Hans Christian Oersted (1777-1851) discovered how a magnetic field is produced during the transmission of the current. Michael Faraday (1791-1867), also a scientist, found that introducing a wire to the magnetic directs the electrical signal through the wire. As one researcher explains, "an alternating current in a (primary) conductor, because of the constantly changing direction of the current, and thus constantly changing the direction of the magnetic field, will induce a similar current in a nearby (secondary) conductor. In the transformer, the conductor wires are formed into coils to enhance the magnetic field and induction effects, and by varying the ratio of turns in the primary and secondary coils, the transformer can be used to change the voltage in the secondary." Westinghouse's employee, William Stanley came up with a workable transformer in 1886.

For the Niagara electrification project, Westinghouse was chosen by the Niagara Falls Power Company to design the system to generate alternating current. The Vanderbilts, Astors, and Morgans provided financing to build large underground conduits that would send electricity as far away as Buffalo. Edison chafed at being shut out of the project.

Love, Marriage and Seminole Lodge

The widower Edison was accomplishing his myriad scientific feats, all the while trying to manage the care of his three small children. Luckily, he met and married a well-educated and highly competent woman.

Thomas' second wife was the daughter of a successful, paradigm-shifting inventor. Born to Lewis Miller and his wife Mary, young Mina (one of 11 children) was groomed to respect ingenuity and education, qualities that served Edison well when the time came to ask for Mina's hand in marriage. Lewis Miller was an excellent student and later teacher, and he invented improvements to agricultural tools and machines that would push the farming industry into the 20th century. Miller also believed both public and church-lead education systems were flawed and needed reform. The Millers were wealthy enough to wield influence, and Lewis Miller achieved much of what he hoped, both personally and professionally.

In 1885, after a relatively typical coming of age, successful high school career, and 'Grand Tour,' Mina began to attend Miss Johnson's, a finishing school for young ladies in Boston, Massachusetts. Close friends and business colleagues of Edison's,

Mr. and Mrs. Ezra Gilliland of Boston, recognized their friend was floundering as a bachelor and set to work to find him an appropriate match. Although Edison is reported to have enjoyed the company of women, he may not have been ideal husband material. He frequently had foul breath and dandruff, and he was known to have dressed carelessly for a man of his station in life. Also, his deafness caused him to shout, and to lean in uncomfortably close when talking. He abstained from alcohol and said, "To put alcohol into the human body is like putting sand in the bearings of an engine. I am a total abstainer from alcoholic liquor. I always thought I had a better use for my head." He was a known workaholic, long before the term existed. Still, he must have possessed some charms, because in 1885 Mina Miller agreed to become his wife when he proposed to her using Morse code.

In 1886, the newlyweds moved into a home called Glenmont in Llewellyn Park, New Jersey: one of the first planned suburban communities in the U.S. Founded by Llewellyn Solomon Haskell in 1853, the former woodland and farming area was transformed into a picturesque community of fine estate homes surrounded by carefully planned natural and cultivated landscaping. The neighborhood likely appealed to Edison's futurist tendencies. The idea there could be an ideal community that was carefully planned and designed for wealthy city dwellers looking for a home in the country was perfect for Mina and Thomas. The 29-room, Queen Anne Style home was decorated and furnished by a well known interior designers, Pottier & Stuymus, in keeping with the Edison's social aspirations. The home featured the firm's Gothic Style, combined with decorative arts and Victorian age furnishings. Hand-stenciled walls complemented the first-floor library with its ceiling height cabinets, fully stocked with leather-bound books. Throughout the home, every effort was made to emphasize good taste and status. The Edisons were keen supporters of the arts, and they reveled in displaying their investments in culture. No expense was spared in bringing in Persian Rugs, major works of painting and sculpture, clocks from Tiffany and Co. and fine French porcelain to grace the halls and rooms of

Glenmont. The home also exemplified modernity and featured marvels such as hot and cold running water, a central heating system, and a refrigerator room in the kitchen. Edison had the home wired for direct current electricity soon after he purchased it and powered the lights with a line that ran directly from his lab in West Orange.

Early that year, Edison had traveled to Fort Myers, Florida to recover from an illness exacerbated by the chilly northern climate. In the balmy sun-drenched south, Edison built a winter retreat for his soon-to-be wife, Mina. He purchased acreage, complete with a small clapboard shack, and developed the property into an elegant place to holiday away from the New Jersey laboratory. He dubbed the property *Seminole Lodge* to honor the local native tribe. Located on the bank of the Caloosahatchee River, the site was ideally suited for Edison to build a laboratory, a house, guesthouse, and other buildings to meet the needs of his growing family. It suited him in other ways as well; having first been attracted by the naturally growing bamboo on his property (which he was using to improve light bulb filaments), and seemed to have all the qualities the inventor was looking for in property.

Edison was keenly interested in botany. He appreciated plants for their potential industrial uses: an interest he'd put to good using during wartime, but he also had an eye for beauty. The retreat would eventually boast a rose garden, moonlight garden, as well as a botanical research garden (later known as the Edison Botanical Laboratory) with more than one thousand plant and tree varieties from around the globe. In the late 1920s, Edison would work closely with his friend and neighbor Henry Ford to identify a plant that could be a source of domestic rubber. At the time, all rubber was imported, and both Edison and Ford realized that should trade be cut off, due to war, or another international crisis, many of their industrial interests could fail. Edison, Ford, and another colleague, Harvey Firestone formed the Edison Botanic Research Corporation in 1927. After testing close to 17,000 plants, Edison identified the plant *Solidago edisoniana,* or Goldenrod, as a potential source of the latex necessary to produce rubber. During WWII, a synthetic version would take the place of natural rubber.

Edison's War Work

WWI set in motion new directions for Edison's work. On April 6, 1917, the United States declared war on Germany, joining Britain, France, and Russia in an alliance. Edison was 67 years old in 1914. Working feverishly in his New Jersey laboratory, Edison's innovations had, until that point, primarily served civilian needs. However, when it became apparent that Germany's U-boats could undermine the success of the Allied forces by keeping merchant vessels on the run, Edison stepped up to assist. The sinking of the Lusitania in 1915 also impelled Edison to action. The New York Times interviewed Edison that year, and he explained, "Science is going to make war a terrible thing – too terrible to contemplate. Pretty soon we can be mowing down men by the thousands or even millions almost by pressing a button."

Edison recognized enormous gaps in America's preparedness for war. The *New York Times* reported Edison was calling for a massive research effort to be undertaken. His vision would include military, civil and political participation, and its goal would be to "take advantage of the knowledge gained through this research work and quickly manufacture in large quantities the most efficient and very latest instruments of warfare." Working within the tightly laced structures of the American naval hierarchy would prove a significant challenge for freewheeling Edison, but his contribution was notable.

A few years before the outbreak of war, Edison visited Europe for a holiday and sightseeing tour with his family. Not intended as a work or promotional trip, admirers mobbed Edison in Britain, France, Austria, Switzerland, and Hungary. Upon returning to America, the *Miami Metropolis* interviewed Edison, and he revealed a series of predictions for what the world may become 100 years hence. During his holiday, he had witnessed significant changes in the popularity and application of steam in industry and transportation and predicted that steam would gradually give way to other types of power sources. Notably, he predicted high-speed electric train travel. He also believed air travel would become more than just a dangerous novelty, but a swift and convenient means of public transportation. Edison thought new processes for refining metals into lightweight steel would result in new uses for the material. He said, "The baby of the twenty-first century will be rocked in a steel cradle; his father will sit in a steel chair at a steel dining table, and his mother's boudoir will be sumptuously equipped with steel furnishings."

His hopeful attitude towards technological potential was often accurate, but sometimes he overestimated its influence and promoted ideas that were more fanciful than plausible. He predicted, for example, that because of technical developments poverty would be eradicated by 2011. His predictions of warfare were notable in their accuracy. He saw that in the future, nations would stockpile armaments, making warfare either impossible to consider, or a final, devastating event.

When war did begin in Europe, Edison reacted with horror and concern. It was, he said, against his nature to contribute his inventiveness to the project of killing; "Making things which kill men is against my fiber. I leave that death-dealing work to my friends the Maxim brothers." (The Maxim Brothers were American inventors who caused Edison no end of trouble with patent disputes; they claimed the electric light bulb was their invention). Despite his moral hesitation, Edison felt that organizing military preparedness in an industrial model could improve chances of Allied victory.

Still, the war had an impact on Edison's work. In his Orange, New Jersey factory, the materials he needed to produce phonograph records, namely phenol or carbolic acids, were cut off by the embargo. The alternative, widely critiqued by his competitors, was to create the acids from American coal, but no manufacturing facility yet existed, and chemical developers and manufacturers were reluctant to undertake the project. Edison, like a dog with a bone, compelled his staff to begin working on developing a new process to produce synthetic phenol. He had a plant built and fully operational, and within a month was generating tons of very high-quality phenol. Later, this same factory would produce other essential chemicals for industry. Wartime reduced supply of many essential products and Edison's work significantly filled the gap.

Edison had previously demonstrated an interest in naval technology, working on torpedoes during the 1890s and the Spanish-American war. He even invented a weapon that would spray electrified water onto the enemy. It was an ingenious, but cruel idea; fortunately, the weapon never went into production!

Edison's primary interest, regarding naval warfare, was to convince the American Navy to replace their lead-acid batteries with his alkaline storage batteries. In 1915 an F-4 Naval submarine sank and lost all hands. Edison was convinced beyond all doubt that a faulty, dangerous lead-acid battery was responsible for the incident. The alkaline battery, while efficient, and much safer than lead-acid batteries, was far more expensive to produce. He enlisted a friend and fellow inventor Miller Reese Hutchinson to promote the alkaline battery to the American Navy. One reporter for the *New York Times* was convinced and in 1915 wrote, "Edison, the man opposed to war and its implements has perfected a battery that will not only make the submarine habitable by preventing asphyxiation of the crew... but will practically double the strategic efficiency of the submarine craft." The American Navy also recognized the merits of the newer technology and ordered Hutchinson to proceed with fitting their submarines with Edison's batteries. When Edison was notified by telegram of this important success, he replied: "I thought I was some optimist, but your telegram will cause the boys around here to lash me to the machinery to keep me from flying." Unfortunately, the battery would later be responsible for a devastating accident, resulting in the deaths of five men. Courts found that safety procedures had not been followed correctly, but a suit was brought against Edison, and the debacle cost him $66,000 to settle.

The Secretary of the Navy, Josephus Daniels, joined Edison in forming a Naval Consulting Board to provide technical advice and support to the Navy during wartime. Both Daniels and Edison were wary of Naval protocol and had little patience with the formalities the Navy imposed, and Edison believed military men lacked imagination. After the war ended, he remarked, "I made about 45 inventions during the war, all perfectly good ones, and they pigeon-holed every one of them. The Naval officer resents any interference by civilians. Those fellows are a closed corporation." This was a characteristic of Edison's personality – he wanted to be in charge, and chaffed when he was not. Daniels was better at playing the game, but in fact, naval higher ups scoffed at Daniels' concept of an advisory committee for invention, chalking it up to his already dubious reputation as a crackpot. When the new board was planning one of its first meetings, even Franklin Delano Roosevelt bypassed the invitation saying, "Tomorrow the inventors come in force, but I am dodging the trip to Mt. Vernon. Most of these worthies are like Henry Ford, who until he saw a chance for some publicity free of charge, thought a submarine was something to eat!"

Edison was named the president of the new Naval Consulting Board, but another individual, William H. Saunders was appointed to chair the meetings due to Edison's deafness. Edison was able to keep up during the sessions by having his friend and colleague, Hutchinson, use Morse code to 'live stream' the discussion by tapping on Edison's knee. The board was made up of scientific and industries luminaries such as Willis R. Whitney of the General Electric

Research Laboratory, Howard E. Coffin of the American Society of Automotive Engineers, Arthur Compton and Robert Millikan, physicists and future Nobel Prize winners, among others. Edison, although known to be prickly, made a positive impression on many board members. Millikan reportedly said that Edison's "ears were gone, but there had been no crystallizing of his mind, such as occurs with some of us before we are born; with others, especially with so-called men of action, before we are forty; and with most of us... by the time we are 70." Edison was 76 at the time.

The 'Edison Board' began its work with no staff, legal status, or budget but due to wide publicity, and the association of the board's activities with so many famous individuals resulted in a deluge of 'suggestions' for ways to improve the Navy's performance. They established a New York office and reviewed hundreds, and eventually, hundreds of thousands of concepts mailed in by amateur inventors nationwide. Edison's laboratory concept received funding to the tune of one million dollars but wasn't constructed until after the end of WWI. Disagreements about where to locate the facility rankled. Edison preferred Sandy Hook, which would place it near his other facilities, but most of the board members thought Annapolis a more practical choice. The spot south of Washington would take the prize, but soon after Edison lost faith in the project noting, "I am convinced that it will ultimately be controlled by Naval Officers, that its position at Washington will always be a handicap, and that it will be an expense to the government without producing any practical results." He'd be proved wrong, and the very same laboratory would one day develop the critical wartime tool: radar. Edison resigned from the board in 1920 but continued to work at solving military problems.

Edison's wartime work on submarines produced essential developments. He began by seeking to acquire as much knowledge as he could about the German U-boats but was often frustrated by the lack of data available. In 1917, he learned that no concrete data about ship sinking had yet been compiled and examined, and undertook to pull together a report on his own. Edison's work revealed submarine activity was focused primarily on established shipping lanes, close to the major ports in both Britain and France. He recommended that ships attempt a transit of the English Channel only during darkness and felt the density of traffic was a problem that could and should be adjusted. Furthermore, he suggested that ships rely more heavily on the use of soundings and charts to determine their positions, and avoid reliance on lighthouses and coastal features, resulting in routes much more accessible for German submariners to track. Edison also thought allied ships were too visible to the enemy, and suggested unused masts be cut down completely, smoke funnels shortened, and that a less smoke-producing type of coal be substituted for the boilers. Edison's seemingly boundless imagination was responsible for many suggestions, but it's unclear if any were ever employed.

Gunnery was also within the range of Edison's experimentation. He was concerned about how to prevent rust in Naval guns and sought to improve the accuracy of projectiles into the water. To aid in his experiments, Edison managed to get his hands on a submarine, the S.P. 192 – a patrol boat. He uprooted his family, moving to Connecticut to test some of his theories and inventions. Mrs. Edison was not pleased with this turn of events. In a letter to her son, she complained, "I detest it on the boat and long to be home. I wish I knew just how much and what Papa wants me out here for... the more cluttered the place, the more contented Father seems to be. I could kill Hutchinson for ever getting him into this mess." Still, Edison continued his experiments, testing new types of sea anchors, and various methods for preventing ships from sinking when struck by torpedoes or deflecting them altogether. Submarine detection was another concern, and Edison enjoyed working on the problem, even though it baffled him at times. He'd have some success, but would eventually be outdone by Willis Whitney (an advisor at General Electric) and Lee De Forest (a radio and telegraph expert), and it was reported that Edison was gracious in defeat and impressed by his colleagues'   work.

Edison and Anti-Semitism

Between the years of 1914 and 1924, Edison and three of his closest friends: Henry Ford, Harvey Firestone, and John Burroughs, spent summers together camping in various scenic locations around the country including the Adirondacks, Appalachia, and the Everglades. They called their group 'The Four Vagabonds,' and the epic campouts often involved an entire fleet of Ford motorcars, servants, and even a table large enough to seat 20! Each man had an assigned role. Edison was the map-bearer and navigator, which suited his desire to control their explorations to some degree. Firestone took care of food (and the cooks to prepare it), Ford oversaw the vehicles and any mechanical difficulties that arose, and Burroughs, a naturalist, provided bird and plant identification on their frequent ambles. The trips were part lark; the men liked to swim, chop wood, and sit around the campfire discussing philosophy, science and politics, and part publicity stunt, with frequent stops for photo opportunities and interviews with local journalists. The trips became such a spectacle that eventually they had to be discontinued.

Edison had a close friendship with Henry Ford: a known anti-Semite, but does that imply that Edison possessed anti-Semitic views as well? Evidence on the topic is mixed, but a brief examination of the context surrounding anti-Semitism is revealing. Stereotypes and discrimination of Jewish people were systemic and pervasive in Europe for centuries. In America, anti-Semitism arose in the late 1800s and was promoted by the Ku Klux Klan, and by Henry Ford, who opposed WWI and believed Jews orchestrated the war for profit. He also believed Jews made little contribution to society and that the stereotypical Jewish financier was a criminal who deserves to be removed.

Ford promoted his anti-Semitic ideas through his publication *The Dearborn Independent*. His attitude was unequivocal: "Jews are the scavengers of the world. Wherever there's anything wrong with a country, you'll find the Jews on the job there." Edison and Ford first met at a conference in 1896. Ford had admired Edison, and the new friendship was deeply satisfying to him. Edison was impressed with Ford's work on a gas-powered car and knew it would be a success. It was the first genuine encouragement that Ford had ever received, and it meant the world to the young businessman. In later years, the two giants of the industry would frequently travel together, and Ford eventually purchased property next door to Edison's Florida estate. It was widely reported the two gave each other expensive gifts. It seems impossible they could be so close without sharing political views, but the evidence is contradictory. Like many, Edison believed there was a connection between Jews and Communism: the most hated political ideology of the time. A somewhat contradictory perspective: that Jews were innately capable of making money was another belief that Edison shared with many. He once wrote, "I wish they [Jews] would all quit making money." However, Edison also recognized that Jews were a much-persecuted minority, and looked forward to a change in their status. In response to a letter from the American Jewish Congress requesting his support, Edison replied, "I am in favor of having a Jewish Congress, as well as any other device that Jews can think of, to obtain their rights. I believe the day is not far distant when men will not be persecuted for wanting to go to Heaven in their own way and not in some other people's way." Edison also employed Jews, though not in great numbers, and even featured a photograph of Jewish banker Otto Khan on the wall of his laboratory. Khan had cleverly re-organized railway transportation systems in America and was a builder and patron of the arts well known in New York and beyond. One Russian-Jewish scientist who worked for Edison argued that his employer was no more prejudiced than anyone else: "It was difficult for any Jew to get a job, so restricted were the laboratories. But Edison didn't care who you were, as long as you were a good worker." Unfortunately, some evidence suggests otherwise. Edison's wealth partly financed the Institute for Historical Review, an organization that sought to deny the holocaust ever happened. Also, many of Edison's sample films featured 'comic' stereotypes of Jews as crafty, cunning, and burdened with large, ugly noses. *Cohen's Fire Sale* (1907) is one example, in which the Jewish shop owner appears to give a poor, cold beggar a brand new, warm coat for free. When the beggar walks away from the shop, we see SHOP AT COHEN'S emblazoned across the back.

In fact, Edison's aggressive foray into filmmaking had pushed many Jewish producers and directors, including Carl Laemmle (founder of Universal Pictures), out of the east coast industry. Edison expected to receive royalties from individuals who were using *his* technology to make films, and more than 200 lawsuits were filed on behalf of his Motion Picture Patents Company. *The Trust (*as the company was known to insiders), gave rights to cooperating filmmakers to use Edison's cameras and granted the Eastman Kodak Company a monopoly on producing the film for them. Before long though, a new way of creating short, inexpensive films emerged: The Nickelodeon, and many of Edison's Jewish competitors found a gap in The Trust and courted the movie-houses with the popular and sometimes off-color short films. This gave Edison even more fuel to fire his dislike of Jews. He claimed his films would uphold the moral integrity of society and the Nickelodeons and later, Hollywood films were morally corrupt. By this time though, it was too late for Edison to take the day. The industry had moved west, and was by-and-large owned and controlled by a very wealthy and thriving Jewish community.

In correspondence with author and Jewish historian Isaac Martens, Edison wrote, "The Jews are certainly a remarkable people, as strange to me in their isolation from all the rest of mankind as those mysterious people the Gypsies. While there are some 'terrible examples' in mercantile pursuits, the moment they get into art, music, and science, and literature, the Jew is fine."

In 2015, the State of Israel had planned to release a postage stamp featuring an image of Edison. The release was halted when it was discovered that many still believe Edison was an anti-Semite.

The Electric Chair

Most famously, Alternating Current was used (disastrously) to operate the first electric chair. In 1888, Edison published a scathing rebuke of A/C titled, "A Warning." Edison truly believed A/C was a deadly technology, and this was partly what motivated him, but he also knew his time to sell D/C as the superior choice of electrical transmission systems was running out. One factor was the ever-increasing price of copper that began around 1887. D/C required the use of thick copper conductors to transmit a current, and while A/C also used copper, it was in far smaller quantities. Put simply, Westinghouse's agents could offer electrical service at a far lower price than Edison's. At one point in the battle for market share, Westinghouse graciously offered Edison an olive branch, suggesting in a letter that they create a Westinghouse/Edison merger. Displacing blame for their feud onto others, Westinghouse wrote, "I believe there has been a systematic attempt on the part of some people to do a great deal of mischief and create as great a difference as possible between the Edison Company and the Westinghouse Electric Co. when there ought to be an entirely different condition of affairs." Edison responded with hostility and accused Westinghouse of exaggerating the superiority of A/C.

It was merely a coincidence that concurrently, the New York State

Legislature was investigating methods for executing criminals. Hangings were deemed inhumane and ineffective as a deterrent. Other methods – including the firing squad, were unpalatable to an increasingly sensitive public. For the first time, different methods of rehabilitation for criminals, and views on justice were shifting. Whereas previous generations had viewed revenge, or an eye for an eye, as an appropriate response to a breach of the law, the 19th century brought with it an understanding that only very few crimes, or criminals, were irredeemable, and that many crimes had social causes. For the recidivist or incorrigible criminal, the execution was perceived as a mercy, rather than a punishment. Edison saw electric shock as an answer to providing a palatable death to such criminals. He stated death could be rendered "in the shortest space of time, and inflict the least amount of suffering upon its victim." The promise of "instantaneous death" (in Edison's own words) appealed to the public, and Edison came up with several monikers for the process in response to a New York Times call for suggestions. Edison's ideas included *dynamort* and *ampermort* and other terms that employed the Latin suffix 'mort' meaning death.

A curious aspect of Edison's personality was that as much as he desired the financial rewards of success, he cared equally about beating out his competition, no matter the contest. "I don't care much for the fortune" he once remarked, "…as I do for getting ahead of the other fellow." He pulled no punches. Calling out his competitors as careless, their materials as cheap, and their use of his filaments as blatant theft, Edison appealed to industry leaders and the public with equivalent zeal. The electric chair presented an opportunity for Edison to show, in dramatic fashion, the superiority of his inventiveness, and of the D/C system.

Scientific American was one of the first respected publications to feature electricity as a means of bringing about intentional death. In an 1883 article titled "Killing Cattle by Electricity," the authors argued that electricity, correctly applied, could bring about painless death. The interest in creative applications for electricity reflects a general wave of interest in finding scientific solutions for social problems. The science of society had become a widespread phenomenon during previous decades. Individual theorists began to recognize cultural and societal impacts on human behavior. Economics, politics, biology, and social structures were all placed under a scientific and theoretical lens, and in dramatic contrast to the past, scientific theories were embraced publicly, even in the face of religious and moral condemnation.

Initially, Edison opposed the death penalty altogether. Writing to the inventor and dentist Alfred P. Southwick, he stated he didn't think anyone had the right to kill another human being. As Southwick's idea for an 'electric chair' gained popularity though, Edison changed his tune. Not only had he recognized the necessity of finding a humane way to execute prisoners, but he also saw an opportunity to spark a new campaign against Westinghouse and Alternating Current. In a letter penned to Southwick in 1887, he said, "The best appliance in this connection is, to my mind, the one which will perform its work in the shortest space of time, and inflict the least amount of suffering upon its victim. This, I believe, can be accomplished by the use of electricity, and the most suitable apparatus for the purpose is that class of dynamo-electric machinery employing intermittent currents. The most effective of these are known as 'alternating machines,' manufactured principally in this country by George Westinghouse... The passage of the current from these machines through the human body, even by the slightest contacts, produces instantaneous death." Edison once again demonstrated his ability to undermine an opponent, while maintaining his reputation and popularity. He understood that for D/C to become the world's preferred electrical system, he would have to demonstrate that D/C was the safer option. What better way to accomplish this than by insisting that A/C was a deadly killer! In 1887, Edison went so far as to demonstrate a public execution of a dozen animals: dogs, cats, and horses using a 1,000-volt A/C generator attached to a metal plate.

Edison's support for electrocution likely influenced the Gerry Commission. Formed in 1885 by New York Governor David Bennett Hill, the legislative commission was charged with identifying a humane alternative to hanging. They met with numerous experts, conducted surveys, and carefully researched numerous methods of execution including gas, beheading, lethal injection, poisoning, stabbing, hanging, electrocution and multiple others in terms of their physical effects and efficacy. They also sought to clarify the purpose of execution. Their findings identified two primary objectives. The first, punishment of a criminal should not inflict cruel and unusual punishment. The report stated, "The deprivation of life is, in itself, the most serious loss which any human being can suffer." Secondly, they determined to restructure the entire process of execution. Ultimately, the commission made a series of recommendations including the abolishment of hanging to be substituted by "a current of electricity, of sufficient intensity to destroy life instantaneously, be passed through the body of the convict."

Edison was pleased and even more determined to sabotage A/C and his rival, Westinghouse. He secretly supplied funding to Southwick, the electrical engineer selected to design for the electric chair, to ensure that it would use A/C. Edison was confident the result would be disastrous, and he was not far from wrong.

On August 6, 1890, convict William Francis Kemmler was the first individual to be put to death by electrocution in New York State. Kemmler, a peddler, and alcoholic from Buffalo had been found guilty of killing his girlfriend, Matilda (Tillie) Ziegler, with a hatchet. By all accounts, the Auburn Prison execution was a horror. After the first shock of 700 volts was applied, the current failed, and Kemmler was still gasping for breath and twitching. A second shock of 1,030 volts was applied for two minutes. Smoke emitted from Kemmler's scalp; his body had essentially caught fire! An electrode attached to the back of Kemmler's neck was found to have burned through to his spine. Kemmler was dead, but the merciful death that was the single promise of electrocution had failed.

Westinghouse had always objected to the use of his dynamo for the purposes of execution, but Edison had persisted testing and retesting electrocution on a series of animals in his Menlo Park lab. After the event, Westinghouse stated, "They would have done better with an axe," neatly summarizing much of public reaction.

The Next Generation of Edison's

Edison and Nancy Stillwell's daughter and first child, Marion Estelle (Dot), was born in 1873. She once said of her famous father that his "work always came first." When her father remarried after the death of her mother, Marion found herself often in conflict with Mina, who was also a very young woman and now her stepmother. The dynamic created a rift between Marion and her father, who'd previously been close, and Marion felt that Mina had taken her place in the family. After completing her boarding school education in New Jersey and Massachusetts, Marion spent much of her adult life in Europe, she survived a seven-week battle with smallpox. During the illness, she'd received only two letters from her father, and felt slighted and hurt by his inattention to her plight. In 1895, Marion married a German army officer, Oscar Oeser. The couple held differing views on the war, and their marriage ended in divorce in 1919. Marion, like many Edisons, lived to a ripe old age of 93 and died in 1965.

Edison's second child, Thomas A. Edison, Junior ('Dash') was born January 10, 1876. He was only eight years old when his mother, Mary Stillwell passed away. It's certain that Thomas Jr. had little contact with his busy father, and as a youngster was raised by relatives. In his early teens, he attended boarding schools in Concord, New Hampshire and Staten Island, New York, and was only a middling success at his studies. While at school, he maintained a correspondence with his new stepmother, Mina, and seemed to be unusually close to her perhaps due to their closeness in age. She would have been in her mid-twenties, as he was becoming a young man. He left school at 17 and took work in his father's failing mine, never taking on more than menial jobs. He drank to excess, and in some of his correspondence with school friends, he seems to suffer from symptoms of psychosis. He married for the first time in 1888 and divorced a year later. In 1906, he married Beatrice Hayzer, a nurse who'd cared for him during a 'serious illness' a few years prior. Thomas Jr. tried to profit from the Edison name with several schemes including remedies and inventions, including a 'better' light bulb, 'Wizard ink tablets,' and a lamp that would use ocean waves to generate electricity, but he didn't have his father's knack with either invention or business. His inventions were duds, and his father complained in *Life Magazine*, "I am thinking of a scheme to prevent persons from using the name I have striven honorably to protect." Thomas Jr. even promoted an electrical device called the *Magno-Electric Vitalizer,* promising a cure for almost any ailment, including rheumatism, deafness, and menstrual symptoms, but it barely functioned, and certainly provided no cures. Eventually, The Edison Sr. filed a court injunction to prevent further use of his name calling his son "absolutely illiterate scientifically and otherwise." He also had Thomas Jr. agree to accept a modest allowance in lieu of being wholly disowned. During this period, he lived with Beatrice under an assumed name and operated a mushroom farm. Now in his 30s, Thomas Jr. became increasingly depressed and continued to drink heavily. He returned briefly to work for the Edison laboratories, primarily due to efforts of his brother and even sat briefly on the Edison Co. board of directors. Sadly though, Thomas Jr. died under somewhat mysterious circumstances, possibly suicide but undoubtedly hastened by his alcoholism.

William Leslie Edison was born in 1878 and was 2 years younger than his closest sibling, Thomas Junior. Like his older brother, William's relationship with his father was strained. After completing boarding school and attending Sheffield Scientific School at Yale, he participated in both the Spanish-American War in 1898 and the First World War where he was a sergeant in the U. S. Army Tank Corps in England and France.

After his discharge, he rejected his father's life of scientific inquiry and instead became a chicken farmer. Edison once said of William, "I see no reason whatever why I should support my son. He has done me no honor and has brought the blush of shame to my cheeks many times."

Edison's three children with Mina Miller were all born at the Glenmont Property. The first, Madeleine was born in 1888. Nicknamed 'Toots,' she later attended Bryn Mawr College where she demonstrated exceptional intelligence. Little is known of her relationship with her father. In 1914, she married aviator John Eyre Sloane in her parent's drawing room. The elder Edison's were not pleased with her choice, because John was Catholic. The marriage produced four grandchildren for Thomas and Mina. Madeleine ran for Congress in 1938, and later she took over care of the Edison birthplace in Milan, Ohio. Madeleine died February 14, 1979.

In August 1890, Charles Edison was born. This was the same year that his father formed the Edison General Electric Company. After an early career operating a little theatre, Charles married Carolyn Hawkins in 1918. His father disapproved of the theatrical life, and brought him into the family business, beginning with a job in Edison Records. Charles presided over Thomas A. Edison Inc. starting in 1927. He also had an impressive political career and was made Governor of New Jersey in 1940. He was mostly responsible for creating the charitable organizations that bear the Edison name, including the Charles Edison Fund (formerly The Brook Foundation), and the Charles Edison Youth Fund later renamed The Fund for American Studies. He died in 1969 at age 78.

Theodore Miller Edison, the last Edison child was born July 10, 1898. Possibly the child most like his father in temperament, the family called Theodore "the little laboratory assistant." He earned a degree in physics from MIT in 1923 and stayed on as a graduate student. Surprisingly, he was the only Edison child to complete a college-level degree. Theodore married Anna Maria Osterhout in 1925. Interestingly, Anna's father was a Professor of Botany at Harvard and received some public attention when he theorized that adequate nutrition could be obtained from air, water, and sunlight. He worked briefly for Thomas A. Edison Inc., but later formed his own company, Calibron Industries Inc. Like his father, Theodore had many ideas for inventions and earned his first patent at age 33. His inventions included a mapping tool and a device that reduced vibration in machinery. He also shared his father's interest in ecology and put it to good use in attempts to preserve essential woodlands in Florida. In 1992, Theodore died from Parkinson's disease with more than 60 patents to his name.

Edison's Legacy

On October 18, 1931, Thomas Alva Edison passed away in West Orange, New Jersey after two years of steadily declining health. During his lifetime he established more than 100 companies and subsidiaries in diverse industries including mining, railways, telegraphy, phonograph, motion pictures, and electric light. He introduced the idea of collaborative teamwork into the modern workplace and perfected systems for the mass manufacture of consumer goods. He carefully selected employees with expertise in the mathematics and technical skills he lacked. His Menlo Park laboratory complex employed 10,000 workers at its peak.

Shaped by the times, Edison capitalized on the Industrial Revolution, and ushered technology into the modern era. He exemplified the quality of perseverance, both professionally and personally. His family life, including two marriages and six children, also reflected 19th-century society. Although a distant father, he cared for his children and tried to help them on their own path to success.

President Herbert Hoover suggested the following in response to the nation's outpouring of grief at the loss of Edison: "In response to this universal desire to pay personal respect to Mr. Edison's memory, I suggest that all individuals should extinguish their lights for one minute on Wednesday evening, October 21, at 7 o'clock Pacific time, 8 o'clock mountain time, 9 o'clock central time and 10 o'clock eastern time." It seems a fitting tribute to the man who made the lights shine.

Thomas A. Edison had been part promoter, part inventor, and part businessman, but never much of a father. His ideas and business aspirations were of greater importance to him than his relationships. Still, many of the Edison children made reasonably good lives for themselves, and the Edison name has maintained a reputation for respectability and ingenuity. Recently, some of Edison's descendants have protested efforts by the legislature to forestall the development of cleaner and more environmentally friendly light bulbs, noting that their storied ancestor believed in progress and would be the first to embrace the new technology. His great-grandson, David Edison Sloane remarked, "Edison would be inventing a better bulb right now, and he would plan to generate a lot of new jobs and big profits as well as better light." Edison himself once said, "When you have exhausted all possibilities, remember this—you haven't." Often criticized for being a re-inventor: someone who rode on the coattails of others, Edison had his own peculiar talent for seeing flaws and working obsessively to improve and refine concepts and designs to make them functional and to develop streamlined and inexpensive means of manufacture for the inventions that were most in demand.

Indeed, the world owes a debt of gratitude to the unusual man and his exceptional talents.

ABOUT CAPTIVATING HISTORY

A lot of history books just contain dry facts that will eventually bore the reader. That's why Captivating History was created. Now you can enjoy history books that will mesmerize you. But be careful though, hours can fly by, and before you know it; you're up reading way past bedtime.

Get your first history book for free here:
http://www.captivatinghistory.com/ebook

Make sure to follow us on Twitter: @CaptivHistory
and Facebook: www.facebook.com/captivatinghistory so you can get all of our updates!